The great secrets to being prosperous and out of poverty

Author: Luis Arturo Acevedo Acevedo

Thanks

I dedicate this work to my wife Eliana, who supported me at all times, to my parents who always supported me and who sacrificed to give me an education, to my brothers for everything we have lived and fought, to my teachers, who insisted in getting their teachings in my head, my friends, who always encouraged me to carry out this project, and in general to all those who in some way helped me throughout these years, so that I could specify This work, to those who gave me what is necessary to carry out the studies concerning this work that today I dedicate to all of them this book.

I know that these words are not enough to express my gratitude, but I hope that with them, they give to understand my feelings of appreciation and affection to all of them.

INDEX

INTRODUCTION

The first thing that comes to mind is: because the poor do not have money and the rich do have money; But what makes the difference between one and the other is not money; The biggest difference between a rich person and a poor person is their thoughts and attitudes.

The way of thinking and seeing things is what creates the gap between rich and poor. Who thinks as rich has the insured wealth and who thinks as poor has assured poverty and therefore failure.

I'm sure a lot of us have asked ourselves:

Why are there people who reach wealth quickly and legally, and why others cannot get out of poverty, regardless of the opportunities presented to them?

Why are there men and women who cannot reach the payment of the next fortnight with a peso, while some forge wealth that lasts several generations?

This is not due to any kind of ritual or secret that only a few know. The answer lies in "the way of thinking." The rich are rich-minded, the poor are always thinking about the formula to avoid bankruptcy, while the rich think, how do I make this business profitable and successful by winning the maximum possible?

The rich are very clear about their strategy; the important thing is to trust that they have the right to succeed, as much or more than others.

Another difference is that rich people focus all their attention, their thoughts, their emotions and SPEAK on new ideas, projects, businesses and investments. Conversely, poor people think all the time in the lives of others, criticizing negatively, generating gossip and rumors.

The rich man thinks about what other people's habits can be learned to succeed, and the poor man only admires others without taking any action to do what the rich do. Or many times they simply envy successful people with money.

The important thing is to understand that being rich or poor is an apprenticeship, not a condition of birth. Remember that it is possible to adopt a millionaire mentality and one of the ways is to read finance books, talk to financially successful people, and attend seminars and conferences.

It is important to look for new ways to learn and acquire the skills necessary to start a business of your own and be financially independent for financial well-being at work or at school. When we face an opportunity, to impel our mind so that it generates new options of triumph, instead of discarding it thinking that we are not ready to take advantage of it.

We all want to have money and live in abundance. We are fascinated by those who have already achieved it.

We would like to know how they did it and how we could get it.

The only truth is that the difference between the rich and those who are not rich is that the former understand and do the things that others do not understand or do not understand.

The rich follow rules of behavior that have helped them achieve fortune and these rules are what separate them from everyone else.

He has endeavored to codify this behavior so that we can imitate it and improve our financial position.

Specifically, they tell us the following: what people do to earn money; how they continue to win it, in a sort of virtuous circle; how they keep it once obtained; how they spend it; how they invest it; how they enjoy it; and how they donate it in an altruistic way (fortunate they).

THINK OF MONEY

SAVINGS AND INVESTMENT.

Train your brain to be smart with money.

Just as a person can improve in mental abilities to make quick calculations or to be more creative, there is also a way in which you can make your brain help you save money.

Train your brain to be smart with money Train your brain to be smart with money.

Although it helps a lot to have a background in economics, administration, finance or any other area in which the functioning of money is better understood; sometimes it is not enough to develop good financial habits.

This, because most times the wishes do not match the objectives or goals you have when making decisions about expenses: for example, if you get to see a discount on a piece of clothing that caught your attention, In general, he will tend to buy it without thinking much, for two reasons: one, he is in "promotion" and two, he liked it.

It is in this way how many times, even if a person sticks to a budget or is clear when something is need or "taste", sometimes it is simply carried away by those impulses that, equally, does not mean that it will be a fatal financial mistake.

The theme is to be better every day when making decisions and simply can "I can" or "I cannot" easily without having to have remorse or that "little voice" that says inside "nothing happens if ...".

In this regard, the first thing to learn is that money is not an end but a means to achieve happiness: this, with respect to the same source of where or get (your work) to the final destination you will have (purchase). of services or products Once you understand this, all the purchases you make, tend to be more bearable and easier to understand, depending on your needs and priorities.

Previous steps.

Once you have achieved the above, you must begin to make a "total clean" to your finances to start those new habits and thoughts that will help you become smarter in money matters. The first step - and more obvious - is to eliminate any debt you have so far, especially those small credit cards or those that are of less than $ 1 million and you are paying interest. If you have bigger ones, you will have to learn, too, to prioritize them within your new thinking system.

The second is to eliminate all those myths and beliefs about "the bad" of money and its different means of payment or representation. These perceptions are only based on bad advice or bad experiences, but what you need to know is that everything depends of the correct use that you give to all this.

Finally, we must understand that while shopping is something pleasant, it is a procedure that needs to be eliminated as the solution to depression or that "touch of happiness" with which many people assume it. Once the brain understands that purchases are not a stimulus of tranquility or happiness, you begin to eliminate that conception of addictive shopping. And how? Simply talking to yourself whenever a situation of this type arises.

The training.

1. Within what you plan of your budget, you should consider that there are two very important parts that perhaps you have never paid much attention to, but that can make a big change in your perception (and therefore in your behavior) with the money . The first is the savings.

In this, what you have to work on is to stop thinking that, to save, you need to earn a lot. It's false. Begin to develop habits of either $ 100 per day, those coins that are left over from the bus or lunch. When you train your brain to know that those coins are "exclusive" for your savings, everything will start to change.

The second thing is that there must be - almost obligatorily - a percentage of your budget destined for charity or humanity. This means that we must begin to modify the egocentric behavior that money is something for a single person, since with small things (they do not have to be big purchases) it can generate positive experiences for others. This percentage can go between 2% and 10% of your salary, for one or several people. This will help you relate the money to a feeling of gratitude.

2. Perhaps what can cost the most, but it is necessary to do, is to think that it is much better to invest money in experiences than in material goods. For this, what you should always keep in mind is, whenever you want to buy that, the "level of happiness" that you consider that that object or service can give you. Moreover, ask yourself "will you generate pleasant memories?" And this will allow you to discard a large part of the things that are not useful in your life, which, at the same time, you will learn to save more.

The above is based on a theory that you will be able to know better in this note "Money does buy happiness".

3. The credit card is not money. Many people consider that it is a way to get money and pay when they do not

have cash. Then, when you get used to paying that way, you are not aware of what a debt means and you may fall several times before the temptation to buy. Thus, you can develop two options: one, always leaving the card in the house or another, ignoring that the load with you.

This is not about considering that the cards are a bad thing, but it simply knows that this implies its cost (the interest rate) and that it is much more expensive to use it.

4. Set goals and write them down. Having something "tangible" or defined and projecting it can help you be more organized. This goes from the very fact that when he goes out to buy the milk, he writes it on a piece of paper; he will have a reminder that he will only go out and buy the milk. But this also applies if you have savings goals.

When you save "just because", without being aware of why, it will seem a bit absurd and, with that same enthusiasm, you will lose interest. In matters of money, the best thing is to have everything written. Not only is it an old learning technique in which if you write it you understand it, but it also allows your brain to generate a particular projection or vision of how things will be.

With the passage of time, if you adopt these habits, the management of money will be something that begins to be part of your unconscious and your daily routine, helping you to save and make better financial decisions that suit you in every way.

Decide what our definition of wealth is. If we do not have an objective, we cannot assume pretensions. If we do not have a destination, we cannot leave the house. If we do not have a definition of what wealth is for us, we cannot judge or prove our success.

One of the possible definitions of wealth is having enough to not have to worry about having enough. In other words, to feel "comfortable" from the moment we start counting in thousands instead of in euros. That is, to know how much we have, how much we need and how much we can spend up to the next unit of a thousand.

Mark our goals By defining what wealth means for us we already know where we want to go. Setting goals is to mark a calendar to reach the destination. It's like when we drive to a certain place: we need to know at what time we have to leave home; what time we hope to arrive; what path do we have to take; what we are going to do when we get there...

Making money is similar. We have to know in advance what it means for us to achieve wealth, how we try to get there, how long we expect it to take us and what we will be able to do with our money when we get it. Our objective must be realistic, honest and achievable.

Discover what our beliefs are about money and where they come from. We all grow up with myths about money. Many of them come from our parents and the way they educate us. Most of us believe things like money only avaricious and dishonest do; that money corrupts; that happiness and money make bad partners; that, in some way, it is better to be poor; that you are not rich because you do not want to; that you have to work very hard to get rich, etc.

The wealthy do not have any of these tiresome myths about the money that the poor have, either because they have abandoned them or because they have never had them. We should abandon them too, to start with a better chance of getting it. Understand that money makes money. There is no greater truth than this: money makes money. If we spend everything we earn, this rule will never work for us. We have to set aside money for breeding purposes. If we have a rabbit farm and we kill and eat all the rabbits, we will not have any to go on. It is not a complicated science, but it is surprising how many people do not grasp it. When our money starts to reproduce, only then can we reinvest part and spend part, but we cannot spend everything because we will not have more. Therefore, it is convenient that: (a) we set aside some money in order to reproduce it; (b) let's set aside a little to spend; (c) we have to reinvest most of it to form a good and healthy reserve.

Know the difference between price and value. Sometimes we find that a bottle of 100 euros in a luxury restaurant can be found for 5 euros in the store on the corner. This is so because in the restaurant we are not paying only the wine; we are paying for the environment, the service, the situation, the good company, the privacy, the tradition, the food, the elegance and everything that surrounds us. We think we know the price of something, but the value is much more than that. Something is worth only what people are willing to pay for it. A catalog can say that the value of a painting is 500 euros, but that will only be true if someone is willing to pay them. The price of something can be much lower than its real value, for us or for any other person. Or much older. If we want to improve our economy it is worthwhile to study the difference between price and value.

Know how the rich man thinks. If we really want to have our fortune, we have to learn how those who have achieved it think. We need to know their jargon and their language, where they eat and live, how they work and relax how they invest and save. We also need to talk to wealthy people, ask them questions, read things about them (interviews and autobiographies can be full of ideas). In short, we need to study money if we want to increase prosperity.

THE ROAD TO PROSPERITY

Wealth never happens by chance. Always start with a clear goal in mind!

It is only achieved when you have in mind the specific amount of wealth you want to create, so you are forced to create a practical plan and execute it with discipline.

No matter where you are now financially, any goal is possible as long as you use the right strategy.

Below I share some reasons why people are not financially free; they do not achieve their goals because:

They do not know how to manage, maintain and increase their wealth.

They are broken due to a bad financial decision, or they have negative thoughts and beliefs associated with money, which prevent them from attracting more wealth.

If you find yourself facing similar problems, read on to learn how to take control of your financial destiny, attract more money and start expanding your current financial abundance:

1) Re-program your mind to attract more money and expand your financial abundance.

Re-examine the negative feelings you have about money. And start by answering these questions:

What are the negative beliefs that I have around money and the rich?

What will happen if I have more money?

What other beliefs or associations do I have about money?

Next, with each of your negative beliefs, dare to challenge them by asking yourself:

Is this belief true?

Is there a concrete example that makes me think things differently?

Finally, write down all the new beliefs giving them the necessary power to replace the old ones. And every once in a while read aloud each one and let the positive words get recorded in your subconscious mind.

Remember that the blockage of wealth is in your own mind. Destroy that blockage by equipping yourself with a new set of beliefs that will help you advance on your path to financial abundance.

Road to financial freedom.

2) Increase your ability to generate more revenue than ever.

Adding more value to other people's lives is the key to increasing your income and improving your financial well-being. You need to find a way to constantly add real value to people's lives and so you will prosper too.

You can increase your ability to earn more money by expanding your knowledge, skills, and ability to give more to others. When he does, people will start paying more for what he does.

3) Keep, accumulate and grow your wealth.

Always spend less than you earn, and then reverse the difference. It seems simple, but you have to make an extra effort to achieve it effectively. Avoid the temptation to spend everything you earn and choose a percentage of your income to invest each month in something that produces good returns.

Next, develop your own financial freedom plan to intelligently monitor and manage your cash flow. Identify and eliminate all unnecessary expenses and learn how to grow your investments with the help of consulting professionals.

In addition, it is crucial that you have basic training and financial knowledge to help you improve your financial decision making skills in the future. Without a well-defined financial plan, it is very likely to fail financially.

4) Manage and learn to protect your wealth from government and creditors.

It is useless to work hard to build a personal fortune that can be transferred to other hands at any time. Many people have taken decades to build their wealth just to see it destroyed by unforeseen circumstances such as accidents, diseases or unexpected laws.

Get advice from professionals such as lawyers, insurance brokers and accountants, to protect your assets from potential creditors and the government that can take away much of your wealth through a series of taxes you may never have heard of.

5) Enjoy your wealth.

True wealth is an emotion. It is a feeling of absolute abundance. Therefore, do not forget to reward yourself throughout the trip. This also helps you train your brain to get used to believing that making money is an exciting and rewarding journey.

Create a reward plan and start the process of linking sensations of pleasure and emotion as you progress on your path to financial success. Share your success and celebrate with joy, no matter how small your progress is.

Let me tell you this: Changing your beliefs about money and mastering the art of properly managing your finances can be a very rewarding experience in life. So, commit yourself now to walking steadily on your journey to abundance and prosperity!

Before we start we have to know where we are. The first thing we must do is an inventory: check what we already have, what we can use, what we can give up, what we owe, what they owe us and what really constitutes our net wealth.

All we have to do is collect the information: what we owe the bank, what we have in our savings or current accounts or what we owe for the credit cards. Even though our financial situation is not too flattering, it is good to face reality so that we can do something to improve it.

We must have a plan. If the work we have does not give us enough money, we need a plan to generate income in another way. The plan should involve taking financial control of our life. If we have debts or excessive expenses, the plan must include addressing this situation as a priority. The plan could be about a career change, studying a business idea, investing money or generating certain capital to buy a house to rent. Whatever the plan includes, the important thing is to make sure we have one and adjust to it.

Be and look The poor person seems poor. Not because it necessarily has to be so, but because it has a "uniform" that marks it. If you change that uniform, your circumstances will change, because people will react to them differently. We are not far from the great apes and they are related to each other by the way they move and pretend. Those who seem weak and needy are treated as such. The powerful seems reliable. We need to pretend to be powerful and that you can trust us. We have to dress as wealthy and people will think that we are and will treat us accordingly. It is undoubtedly superficial advice, but the rules of money, whether we like it or not, are like that.

If you do not know a person, do not do business with them. If we have the feeling that something, anything, is wrong, it is better that we get out of it. There are unconscious keys that our conscious mind grasps: if we ignore them, we will feel it invariably.

It is good to listen to our intuition: if a situation seems bad, it probably is. If we do not experience the right sensations with the person we are dealing with, it is better to look for a way out.

Learn the art of negotiating. If we are going to negotiate, trade and exchange, we have to learn the art of negotiation. This art basically revolves around making the other person feel that he gets as much as we get. The art of negotiation will help us in many different situations, from getting a simple salary increase to relating with our partners or children. If we learn that art, everything will slide smoothly and easily, we will achieve what we want and others, too. For this reason it is convenient that we have in mind a certain number of negotiation rules:

Always know our limit, the point that we will not exceed.

Always know what we want. Do not negotiate if we do not know what we are negotiating.

Always look for the win-win situation.

Know the importance of each topic: some we can spoil and others, no.

Be prepared always to give in some things to get others, be flexible.

Always know everything possible before you start; In these situations, knowledge is power.

Keep us cold and patient.

Do not make concessions, but negotiate them.

Create more variables (discounts, delivery, payments, terms, etc.).

Find the best deal we can justify. Going down afterwards is easy; Climbing after is almost impossible.

The commercial agreements are great because they give us money. The strategies to close agreements will serve us again and again. We have to learn to be daring, to ask for more, to give what we have for what we want.

Small economies will not make us rich, but unfortunate. Trying to make small economies to become prosperous is something doomed to failure. They will not make us rich, but unfortunate; and feeling miserable is not a good way to start the day. We need a decent breakfast and a positive attitude. Deleting our daily coffee can help us save a few euros and can reduce our intake of caffeine, but it does not make us rich and can make us feel miserable.

The rich do not tighten their belts. Although they spend their money carefully, they do not suppress coffee or buy cheap jam in the hope of getting richer.

Do not waste time thinking, quickly make economic decisions. Getting some benefit for our performance, even if it is small, is better than doing nothing. Although it is not complicated at all, it is surprising how many people overlook it and think: "Later I will decide how to invest that small sum that I have saved, I cannot decide now whether to buy shares or put it in a savings account"; so they do not do anything and their money is still asleep in a checking account.

Doing something is infinitely better than doing nothing. Sometimes, even acting quickly can be much better than waiting for a remote possibility. Let's suppose that we are dedicated to the sale of antiques as a pastime to move our money. If we buy something for 1000 euros and we think we can sell it for 3000, but someone offers 2000 in an hour, it is best to sell it at that time and go buy two more antiques for 1000 euros to sell them in the same way.

Consider the consolidation of debts. It is obvious that, when talking about debts, it is best not to contract them. But if we have already done it, what we need is to pay as little interest as we can while we are paying the debts. Consolidating debts is, in that sense, one of the best options: stop using three or four credit cards, pay the overdraft and consolidate all loans in one. If we decide on the latter, we should take note of some practical advice:

Offer all our creditors to pay them immediately a certain percentage if they cancel the debt.

Never secure anything and under any circumstances against our house. If we do, we could lose it for not paying and there is nothing worth that.

If we have to borrow, it is better to do it against an asset that we can sell (a machine tool, a car) and try not to borrow more than the value of that sale.

Buying on credit is something different. When Jack Cohen set up Tesco, he negotiated to pay the rent for his store with a three-month delay, paid the stock three months later and started to get money at the counter the first day. After three months, he had achieved much more than he should have.

Cultivate a quality that will give us benefits repeatedly. When we do something that nobody else can do (or make as few people as possible), then we can mark our price. It does not have to be a particularly difficult quality, just one that someone wants and is willing to pay for.

We all have something that we can do and that is especially ours, it is with what we think that we can make a fortune just with someone giving us an opportunity. We all have a dream that we can follow, or a plan that we dare to put into practice. That is why we must think about what we have to offer: our capacities, talents and strengths. You do not earn anything thinking all day about your own weaknesses.

Work like a slave to earn a misery. There are many people who work to live and without them the rich could not be richer. This does not mean that workers are exploited or used, only that if people choose to work as a slave and invest all their time and energy in working for a salary, there will always be other people who will overtake them when they see an opportunity and become prosperous, simply for raising your head and looking to the future.

If we are not satisfied with our pay and we hate our job, then we have to question why we keep doing it and what else we can do. The worst possible scenario is that we do not feel fulfilled in our work but we find ourselves so busy with it that we do not have time to create a plan that brings us more prosperity and happiness.

As much as possible, do not rent, but buy. A mortgage can be seen more as an investment than as a loan. If we buy a property with a mortgage, we make a monthly investment. In the long term, we can reasonably expect the interest we pay on our mortgage to be less than the increase in the value of our property. On the contrary, the rent is never an investment and the money spent on it will never be seen again in all safety.

With a mortgage, we have a good long-term opportunity to see that the payments we make to your account result in an increase in the value of our home. When we sell, we get that increase in value.

We must know that, in the long term, real estate property will not be more profitable than transferable securities. Properties and values are the two most popular investment options and it is often difficult to choose between them. However, and despite the momentary problems they may experience, in the long term the values will be more profitable than real estate.

With the shares we expect to have a regular income in the form of dividends that are paid to the shareholders, but their main performance comes, in general, from the long-term increase in its price.

Since companies have more growth potential than real estate, in the long term, stocks should provide us with a higher return. The other reason for preferring securities to mere real estate property is that the shares will allow us to decently diversify the risk, especially when it comes to a well-balanced portfolio. The more variety, the less risk.

Master the art of selling. The sale is the cornerstone on which all fortune is built. Anything we do to prosper will involve a sale: selling our capabilities, things, ideas ... We cannot make money without selling. Everything is in the sale and this is a fact that every rich person knows and does not know any person with few economic resources.

In an ideal world we should pretend to sell the following:

Our capacities, qualities and attributes.

Something while we sleep.

In countries where we have never been and of which we have never heard.

Things that are very cheap to produce and that provide a really healthy performance.

Things that have 99% penetration in all households.

Things that are stored transported and stacked easily.

The sale is not something typical of well-dressed commercials that tell us a beautiful story. Every time Richard Branson goes out on busy television with a hot air balloon, he is selling his entire brand. He is an intelligent man who makes an intelligent sale.

A young student, Alex Tew, wanted to become a millionaire and realized that he would get it if he had a million things he could sell for $ 1. He noticed that a web page has a million pixels. Then he thought about selling each of them to the advertisers for 1 dollar. To be seen, the latter need a block of about 400 pixels, worth $ 400. By Christmas, Tew had already sold half of his pixels and the rest had sold it before finishing the course at the university. The result can be seen at www.milliondollarhomepage.com.

Understand how the stock market really works. John Maynard Keynes once said that the stock market works like a beauty contest. That did not mean that stockbrokers had to change their suits for swimsuits, declare their aspiration to work with disadvantaged children or in favor of world peace; It referred to a type of British beauty pageant that the London newspapers used to organize and through which readers could win an award by choosing the beauty whose photograph was considered the most beautiful by the greatest number of other readers. This means that winning was not about choosing the prettiest, or even predicting which would be the most beautiful according to the average of the readers, but to win.

It became a game of anticipating what would be the opinion of the average reader about the choice of the average reader.

Investors behave in a similar way: they try to earn money by buying securities they think they will want to buy other investors in the future. The price they are willing to pay for a security depends less on the fundamental value of the company than on their expectations that everyone else will be willing to pay for it. This is the essence of speculation in the stock market and, therefore, the fundamental value of an action and its price on a given day can be so different.

However, speculating with the movements of the stock market is not the path to wealth. If we really want to enrich ourselves in it, we have to do it slowly, but surely, through courage. It is convenient, therefore, that we ignore almost everything that is said, the clamor about what it means, referring to a price, this news or that rumor. If we are going to invest in stocks we must look for value, that is, look for companies that do something that people will consider more valuable in the future and whose value is appreciated by investment funds. Once we have found those values, we should buy them thinking about the long term.

Buy only shares (or anything else) that we can understand. If we are going to buy or sell shares, or anything else, it is good that we try to reduce eventualities as much as possible and invest only in what we know and understand well enough. By doing so, we eliminate much of the mystique that can take us more than we pretend and take risks that we would not normally assume.

If, for example, we buy at Marks & Spencer and we see that the new ranges of products are good, that the stores are full and that people are amazed by the way the firm has improved its collection this year, then it is good that let's buy their shares.

If we do not really understand a particular sector and do not intend to work enough on it to know it well, it is better to invest in something else or use an investment fund.

As for the latter, if we do not have the time or knowledge to study the best active fund with attention, it is advisable that we follow the rule that less is more. In general, the funds that do not charge us great emoluments for taking risks with a succession of intelligent strategies to overcome the banking are more reliable. It is advisable to choose those directed by people who are going to invest our money with minimal fuss and emoluments in a good range of values that go with the market. These funds are known as index funds or tracker funds. They are characterized by having a lower broker commission and spending less money on advertising, so your brochure may be the last in the portfolio of our financial advisor. Pay attention to detail. The detail is not to write a note of every small purchase we make and look at the economies to the minute. The detail is the following:

Check the fine print.

Check interest rates.

Check the charges and emoluments.

Check that we pay things on time to avoid incurring penalties.

Check when they pay us to invest it immediately and prevent us from leaving the money.

Do not forget dates, times and appointments.

Make lists and write everything.

INCREASE WEALTH

I will not discover anything new if I tell you that the vast majority of people who inhabit the planet earth want to be millionaires, or at least have enough money that allows them to live without having to develop a job that displeases them just because they need get money to pay their debts.

Many of these people act with the intention of improving their financial situation to be able to access a better life: they acquire more training to be able to aspire to better paid jobs, carry out a job reorientation or, simply, obtain a promotion within their current company. That is, they follow the path traveled by the vast majority of people, a path that does not lead to financial independence but that makes them prisoners of what Robert Kiyosaki once called the rat race: A vicious circle in the that the middle class is involved and that is to work for others in a context like the current one, of taxes on the rise and wages on the downside, to be able to face some long-term debts that were acquired under the assumption that our finances would only go to better. Obviously this way of facing life does not take us anywhere. We can slightly improve our lives and make our obligations more comfortable, but we will never achieve the goal of being financially independent.

The vast majority of people do not reach the level of life they really want because the approach they apply and that is behind the process that I just described is not the right one. Working and trying to prosper in the labor market is just one of the four pillars that we must.

Work to achieve financial independence, but if we leave aside the other three we will only be one more of the herd. And what are the other three pillars on which our personal finances should be based? Patience. Before entering fully into the subject, we need to talk about the key concept that will change your vision about the management of your personal finances.

WHAT IS NET WEALTH?

The vast majority of people measure their financial situation based on the figure that appears on their monthly payroll. Based on that figure (and the expectations of their future evolution) they carry out all their financial decisions, that is, they decide what to consume and how (whether or not to borrow). As you can imagine, wealthy people do not base their finances on obtaining ever larger revenues, among other things because every time our remuneration increases, so do the taxes that we will be forced to pay. If you take a look at the compensation of the CEOs of the most important companies in the world you will see that they are people who do not have an assigned salary, but have a symbolic remuneration. For example Mark Zuckerberg, CEO of Facebook, charges $ 1 a year.

So, how can these people live in the mansions they live in and have the cars they have? They can because their income does not depend on a payroll but on their assets. They are people whose money comes from their assets. Their sources of income are the revaluation of the package of shares they own of their company, rights on licenses, image rights, patents that belong to them ... in short they live on their portfolio of assets and not on their salary.

The key concept that you should keep in mind as of this moment is the concept of net wealth. Net wealth is nothing more than the difference between the value of our assets and our liabilities (Assets - Liabilities = Net Wealth). Thus, if our net wealth is positive, it will indicate that the value of our assets (assets and rights) is higher than that of our liabilities (debts). Our goal from this moment is to build a positive and growing net wealth.

HOW TO INCREASE YOUR NET WEALTH

To increase our net wealth we must act on the two fronts that determine it, assets and liabilities. The first step in any process aimed at increasing our net wealth should be to eliminate all debts that we can, that is, we must put a stop to our liabilities. The first thing you should do is order your debts in the short and long term. Once this is done you must establish a plan to eliminate all the short-term debts that you have assumed (loan for the car, trips, wedding ... whatever). With regard to long-term debts, it is normal that it is a mortgage, which in principle we will not touch. We will continue paying the monthly payments normally, although it is good to analyze with our bank the possibilities of improving the payment conditions. I repeat, the debt that is important to eliminate, since it is the one that does the most damage, is the short-term debt.

Once we have checked our liabilities, we will focus on the other factor that determines net wealth, assets. To increase our assets, we will base ourselves on three aspects other than our salary income: Savings, investment and minimalism.

As we said before, basing our finances exclusively on the salary we receive for our work is an error, but we are going to supplement this income with a system in which the income from work is an important but not unique piece. The key here is to develop alternative sources of income, as passive as possible, that make our monthly income increase. I do not know what your financial situation is right now, but even if you have a good job, well paid, it is always necessary to develop other sources of income. Remember that having a job today is not a guarantee of having it tomorrow. Analyze what you like (write, design, photograph ...) and try to get some income by working as a part-time freelancer. Look for projects that interest you that you can develop in your free time, and try to get hired. The good thing is that you decide how much time you work and, who knows, you may discover your true vocation.

Another fundamental pillar is savings. Many times you have heard that saving is an unwise way to improve our finances. It's true, but only when we save for the sake of saving. Our grandparents were people who saved all their lives. In general, out of fear and ignorance, they never used part of the money that won them so much for any investment product. The result is that they ended their days with very little money. I propose that you save, but from a different perspective: save in order to invest. Saving for saving is an error, it does not work. However, if you save with the objective of obtaining a sufficient amount to allocate it to a financial product or a business project, things change. From now on I suggest that you allocate at least 10% of your monthly income to a savings account every month, and that at the end of the year you allocate the savings to invest well in the markets or to an investment project that interests you (it does not have to be yours, you can finance other people's and become a business angel). In short, use savings as a means and not as an end.

Creating a positive and growing net wealth is not a flower of a day, but it is an objective that every responsible person should have in mind. As you see, the key is to create as many assets as possible, and for that we are going to rely on a system with multiple pieces working as a team: minimization of liabilities, income (assets and liabilities), savings, investment, and simplification of our Lifestyle. Plan periodic goals that are easy to meet and calculate each quarter what your net wealth is, you can create a graph that visually indicates how you are increasing your assets, which will motivate you to move forward.

As you see, it is not necessary that you leave your current job and that you launch yourself into the adventure without a network (which I did and I do not recommend you to do, since it is very hard if you do not have a good financial cushion that I did not have), but you must use your work as a lever to develop the other parts of the system. The time will come to consider the possibility when your income from assets is higher than the income you receive for your work.

Make someone do the things that we cannot do. There are lots of things that have to be done and that we do not know how to do. We could learn, but it is probably not where our talent resides and it is not necessary for us to do so when there are more suitable people out there who can do them. Therefore, we have to do what we are good at and let others do the thing that we cannot, that is, hire really good people and let them deal with the work of making us really prosperous.

In this sense, there are a few rules we must follow to make sure we get and keep the right people:

Know exactly what we want to be done and who we want to do it.

Be very clear what we want to be done for us, how much we are going to pay the people who will do it and the indications we are going to give them.

Keep them informed and motivated, inspire loyalty.

Tell you about our long-term strategy; they also participate in our future, which is also theirs.

If they make mistakes -and they will do it from time to time, we all do it- we have to correct them and continue. Forgiving is good.

Praise them constantly, nothing inspires more than flattery and money.

Mark realistic goals, but do not expect impossible.

Give them a good example: become someone they can respect and in whom they can reflect.

Remember that we are bosses, not friends. Try to maintain dignity, distance and authority.

Find the hidden asset or opportunity. There are always opportunities to make a fortune in our environment.

The only fundamental thing that is required of us is to be open to possibilities.

If we are going to become a "treasure hunter", we only need to "take on board" five things:

The moment is crucial. If we react too slowly, the opportunity will escape us. If we are too fast, we can scare her away. Markets change, fashions vary and products go out of style.

We have to be serious.

Hidden opportunities only become apparent when they feel they are desired. If we want to hunt one, we have to be stealthy, calm and skilled.

We have to be weird. If there are only a few hidden opportunities, we have to excel. Being weird, unique, special, creative, unusual is imperative to stand out from the flock.

We have to know what we do.

To find opportunities and be able to take advantage of them, we need time, dedication and commitment. If we know our subject, we will see the opportunities much more clearly.

Be attractive we have to look good, present ourselves well and radiate attractiveness.

KEEP THE WEALTH

In finance there is nothing more important than generating income. But what to do if in spite of winning you do not have money. Is there a way to conserve money?

For many, money is like water in your hands, it arrives and then it goes away quickly. House payments, food purchases, new shoes ... We never have so much money to not find what to spend it on.

Even if you win well, this still does not guarantee financial stability. If you really want to increase your wealth, you must know how to save and keep your money.

On television, or the Internet tell us the story of Micheal, Tyson and other celebrities who have obtained great wealth, but end in ruin after a few years. What unites all these stories? Bad money management and investments in liabilities instead of assets.

To keep the money you need to be clear about the difference between assets and liabilities. We talk about the concept where:

Active: is everything that makes money enter your pocket.

Passive: is everything that makes money out of your pocket.

Learning from this was a great lesson for me, it helped me to think and reflect on what I am buying. Most of us, without realizing it, invest your money in liabilities. To illustrate it better I show you an example.

Where does all the money go?

Martha and Pablo is a couple who together with their two children live in moderately large homes. She is a teacher and he is a mechanic. Together they earn $ 1300 per month.

The little money left is used for entertainment or unforeseen expenses. Although they do not live with any luxury, at the end of the month they have nothing to save. It is your habit to spend everything you earn.

Now Pablo received a salary increase of $ 200 per month. At the same time, he took with his wife the decision to move to a bigger house.

They sell their current home and their income allows them to obtain a mortgage. Now they live in a bigger house. Their payments for the house grew from $ 300 up to $ 480 per month. Despite their increase, likewise before they have nothing to save.

They have no savings or security fund ... and no cash. Imagine what would happen in case of illness, loss of employment or if the car is damaged. Pablo and Martha can fall into serious financial problems.

We never want to have problems, we do not plan, but things happen and we must be aware of this.

Increase in revenues = increase in expenses.

What happens when we start generating more money? Suddenly you notice that your car is not so new and you need a better one. The house you see small and you need a bigger one. The public school does not meet your expectations, so you send your children to a private school etc.

We want to buy more things, fill ourselves with new obligations and fill ourselves with liabilities. It is the reality we face every day.

By earning more, people start spending more, spending on things they do not really need. Because until now you have lived well without them.

When we do not put a wedge, expenses begin to grow along with the increase in income.

Why is it like that?

We live in a world of consumerism. In all places they tell us that we need something new or something different to be happy. We are attracted with ads of a large television, the latest cell phone model, a perfect car and clothes from the latest collection.

If your salary increases, you will have no problem finding thousands of uses for this money. There is always something that you do not have yet and the world is screaming at you "You need to have it. We want your money! "

How to stop the outflow of money?

Put the financial wedge in use. What is a wedge? It is to determine and maintain expenses at the same level.

If you are earning $ 800 a month and up until now this was enough, to meet the needs of your family, then keep the expenses at the current level. When your income increases it is good to save this additional money.

This does not mean you should not enjoy life. We are not robots whose only objective is to work. We work hard to live better and to enjoy our time here on earth. It is normal that when you earn more you want something "better".

However, do not forget that the more liabilities you have, the more money comes out of your pocket and the more assets you have, the more money goes into your pocket.

Then what should I do?

When I heard the financial wedge method I suddenly knew that "This was my solution". Then I modified it a bit and adapted it for our needs.

According to this method, we nail a wedge in the expenses and all the additional money we get is divided into three groups.

What works for us is:

50% we save, ex. We send this money to a savings account created especially for this purpose;

35% dedicated for personal and work development, ex. We buy books, courses, classes and things that help us in our work;

15% we spend for our wishes, eg. go to the movies, collect money for vacations, buy something new for the house etc.

In this way we can not only keep the money but also feel that we use it in a good way and enjoy what we do.

Take the financial wedge into practice.

Principles of how to conserve money:

Determine the level of monthly expenses that ensure the needs of your family.

Stick a wedge in your spending - keep the cats on the same level. Distribute the additional money between: savings, personal development and entertainment.

Do not buy only liabilities, but also assets that will put money in your pocket. You already know that it is a financial wedge. Are you going to nail her in your expenses? I trust that now you will have more desire to conserve your money. And what to do with the money once when we save it?

It is one of the topics I want to develop later, and if you have not read it yet, I encourage you to learn the difference between passive and active.

Buy quality Buying by quality instead of by price is a difficult lesson that we all have to learn. We have to abandon many of our monetary myths of childhood, such as not spending more than necessary; do not pretend that we buy expensive; not spend money on us, it is wrong; In a way, it's better to get a bargain than buy quality, etc. Buy quality says a lot of things about the way we live, how we behave and how we do business. It also saves us money in the long term, since the cheap often costs us dearly. How to buy. The sensible rich man does not throw money away because he can afford it. Rather the complete opposite: Always ask at least three budgets to do a job and not just accept the first they give.

Go to several stores (or talk to several suppliers) to make sure you are not throwing money away.

He is cautious when it comes to spending when he has to work hard to earn it. It is not miserable, only cautious: it selects and discriminates.

Nowadays, the Internet greatly facilitates the possibility of comparing prices so we should make sure that we do not pay more than we owe for something.

Do not give up capital. If we have to cede participation in the capital of a business, we should make sure that we exchange it for the following:

Capacities and business acumen.

Active participation in management.

An agreement that enables us to run the company in the way we want. A realistic percentage, so that we do not give away too much. A repurchase clause, so that we can buy back the capital, with cash, at a later time, when we have it. In general, we must accept money for our company only from people who have experience in our business and understand the ups and downs and problems related to the sector. In any case, we must not give anybody shares with the right to vote.

SHARE THE WEALTH

There are five secrets based on the behavior of the rich that can help change those attitudes and habits.

The unique characteristics of the rich have been adequate to manage personal and family finances and thus achieve financial freedom.

Is there a relationship between how much a person earns and how to properly manage their money?

Why are there some people who earn little but seem to be able to meet all their financial needs and live comfortably?

Why do other people who earn a lot always seem to be in debt and struggling to solve their problems?

Surely, if you make a lot of money, you must be financially stable. And if he earns very little, he is permanently in debt and struggling with his finances.

The reality is that there is no connection between what you earn and how well you manage your money. Creating wealth for all of us, our families and communities, does not depend on our ability to earn money, but rather on our habits and ability to relate to it.

Financial education is aimed at providing the knowledge and tools around money management. This is one of the documents that are part of the program in which they make an apology.

Here we enunciate some behaviors of these rich that influence the administration of money.

The secret: Pay yourself first and use what remains.

Eat first, before others. You must also "eat first" by making an automatic deduction from your salary or income.

Many people understand that they need to save and save "a little" at the end of the month whenever they can. But this does not work because there always seem to be other expenses that eat this amount.

The first of the five great secrets, reverses this behavior and says "save first" before all other expenses and not at the end of the leftovers. Eat first, before all; you must pay yourself first and save a fixed amount each month. Make this savings an automatic deduction from your salary, before starting to pay other expenses. By first addressing your savings needs, you are securing the future of your own family.

Keep in mind:

Acquire the habit of saving first through an automatic pre-payment mechanism.

Commit to a savings plan.

Define the minimum level of savings that you should have and how to achieve it.

Know the different savings vehicles available.

The Secret forces him to modify his spending habits. Even if you start with a small amount of savings, you will develop a habit of saving. This habit will facilitate the increase of your savings over time. If you practice the Secret, and commit to a savings plan prior to spending, you will be on the right path to real wealth and long-term financial security.

The secret of: Create a financial plan.

Patiently plans and moves towards his goal, never retires or surrenders...

Many savings plans fail because their goals are too vague. Have a very clear idea of what you are saving for.

Keep in mind:

Record and plan precise, clear and specific goals in the short, medium and long term, realistic, achievable and inspiring.

Understand the importance of studying, reflecting, focusing and visualizing your goals and find the best way to support yourself to achieve them.

Use your goals to ensure easier and more consistent financial discipline (for example to help you deal with the impulse to spend for spending).

Remember that the rich always aim for things they can achieve. When he is young he learns first to see easy goals. As you grow and become more experienced, the goals change and become more challenging saving is not easy; you need to have vision, something really inspiring to keep you firm when difficulties arise.

If you have a clear visual image, that will help you "stick to the plan" and achieve your goals with the same determination.

The secret of: Remember how much you earn, know what you owe and what you spend.

The rich never forgets. His power lies in his knowledge, aided by his memory. Remember the places where you have been, and use this knowledge to plan your future.

In knowledge, aided by his memory, lies his power for us, human beings, knowledge is also power.

But since our memory is not so good (especially when it comes to spending), we need to write down what we earn, what we owe and spend to keep us informed and plan our future.

Keep in mind:

Identify different types of expenses and how to manage them.

Develop a family budget at least once a year.

List a simple process to budget that works based on 5 simple steps.

Develop a plan to track variable expenses using the method.

The secret of: Attack and eliminate your debt.

You must evaluate your options. The only option that you do not have is not to deal with the dangers.

.

It is the same with your money. You have to manage the level of debt you assume to make sure it does not threaten your financial security.

The debt you take out should be part of your plan, because it will help you create wealth. But if you do not handle it carefully, you can end up repaying large amounts of your income to the debt through your life thus destroying your wealth.

Because debt is so expensive, and you eat so much of your wealth, we must find ways to reduce it quickly and always handle it with care. The debt is only made unmanageable if you eat a large part of your monthly income and if you pay it too slowly.

Keep in mind:

Plan and manage your debt.

Identify the risks, difficulties, limitations and unforeseen events that affect a budget and explain the consequences of poor financial planning.

Understand how to attack your debt.

Explain the consequences of not having a good credit history in the context of purchases related to credit.

Getting out of debt can be one of the most difficult challenges in life, but it is also one of the most important achievements you can have.

The secret of: Protect your assets and make your money work for you.

It is dedicated to protect and grow your herd knowing that its strength and future lies in its numbers.

Strength and worth are in his family. Although raising a large family takes a lot of patience, in the end it's worth it.

Keep in mind:

Understand why you need to invest to grow your assets.

Have a clear understanding of why you should make sure to protect your assets and inherit wealth from future generations.

Explain the power of compound interest.

Enlist and explain the four financial options to save money and thus ensure long-term financial stability.

Know your rights when dealing with investment brokers, advisors or executives.

It can inspire you to grow your fortune patiently.

It is never too late to start saving, be it for retirement, for the initial installment of a home, for the education of the children, investing in the short term or building a capital for the future. Putting these five secrets into practice will help you to know how to manage your money. The sooner you start the better.

Learn to select works of charity and good causes. Once we have some money, we will be overwhelmed by requests to contribute to charities, support a particular cause or help a particular person. There are, in this sense, a few precepts that we should observe:

Decide what is important to us: the planet, whales, small children, the poor, research in the fight against cancer...

Find out what we want to do: just give money, get involved, advise, ask for funds, etc.

Check on the Internet the charitable works that we can consider desirable and find out if our ideals match theirs.

Check charities: their financial statements, bookings, brochures, campaign information, partners, and mission statements.

Trust our intuition.

When we have achieved it, we should not brag it. The wealth is wonderful. Having money is something big. Getting rich is an activity that is enjoyed and worthwhile.

Handling money well supposes being frugal, restrained with him and without showing off. When we have reached prosperity, we belong to an exclusive club, so we must observe a few rules:

No ostentatious cars.

Nothing of splendor or cockiness.

No compulsive spending.

Nothing to buy islands.

No big diamonds or high jewelry of any kind, because that only attracts thieves.

On the contrary, we should be discreet, with pleasure, refined, educated, for those who are less. Someone we can all look at. Someone who inspires and does not cultivate ridicule. Someone who sets a good example for young people, those who are impressionable and those who do not do things so well.

The boast causes envy, jealousy, criticism, condemnation and censorship, all well deserved. On the other hand, discretion provokes respect, admiration and emulation. It is better that we never mention what.

We have what we value or how much we earn. If we say it, half of people will despise us for not having more and the other half will resent having so much. That information should be provided only to the director of our bank and, even so, it should be he who would have to take that information from us.